*Ali Baba and the Forty Thieves*

# ALI BABA
# AND THE
# FORTY THIEVES

retold by

Walter McVitty

illustrated by

## Margaret Early

CAMBRIDGE UNIVERSITY PRESS
Cambridge
New York  New Rochelle
Melbourne  Sydney

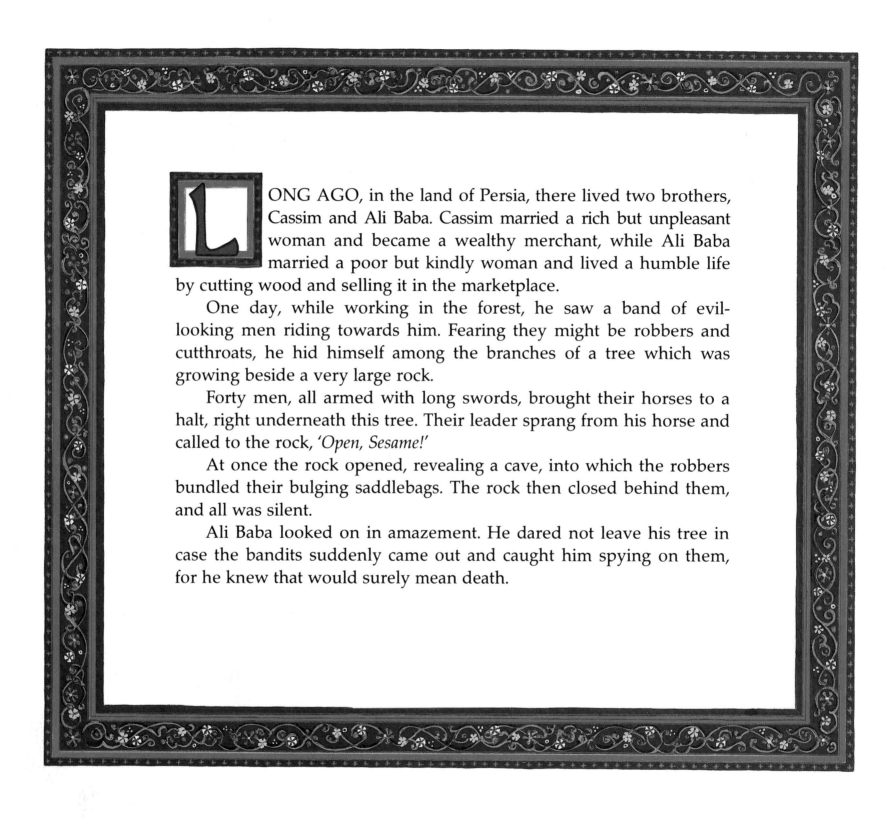

LONG AGO, in the land of Persia, there lived two brothers, Cassim and Ali Baba. Cassim married a rich but unpleasant woman and became a wealthy merchant, while Ali Baba married a poor but kindly woman and lived a humble life by cutting wood and selling it in the marketplace.

One day, while working in the forest, he saw a band of evil-looking men riding towards him. Fearing they might be robbers and cutthroats, he hid himself among the branches of a tree which was growing beside a very large rock.

Forty men, all armed with long swords, brought their horses to a halt, right underneath this tree. Their leader sprang from his horse and called to the rock, *'Open, Sesame!'*

At once the rock opened, revealing a cave, into which the robbers bundled their bulging saddlebags. The rock then closed behind them, and all was silent.

Ali Baba looked on in amazement. He dared not leave his tree in case the bandits suddenly came out and caught him spying on them, for he knew that would surely mean death.

FTER SOME TIME, the rock opened up once more and the forty thieves came out, their saddle bags now empty. As they mounted their horses, their leader raised his hand and called out, '*Close, Sesame!*' The rock closed up once again and the robbers rode off.

Fascinated by what he had seen, Ali Baba climbed down from his tree and stood before the rock. He was curious to see if the magic words would work for him too. '*Open, Sesame!*' he cried, and, behold, the great rock opened at his command.

Trembling with excitement, he entered the cave. The door closed behind him. Instead of being dark and gloomy as he expected, the cave was well lit, for there was a hole in its roof.

Ali Baba was astonished by what he saw. Piled before him was a great treasure — expensive silks, costly rugs, and heaps of gold and silver.

Although poor, Ali Baba was not a greedy man. He quickly filled a few sacks with gold coins, just enough for his two donkeys to carry.

'*Open, Sesame!*' he commanded again, and hurried out. Remembering to say '*Close, Sesame!*' he then led his donkeys home.

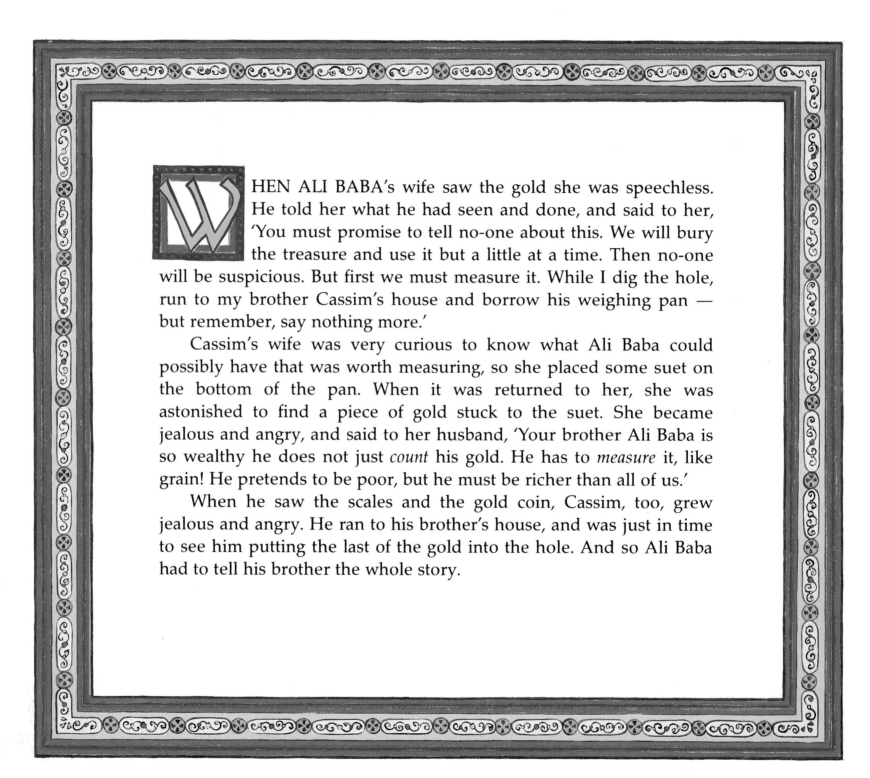

WHEN ALI BABA's wife saw the gold she was speechless. He told her what he had seen and done, and said to her, 'You must promise to tell no-one about this. We will bury the treasure and use it but a little at a time. Then no-one will be suspicious. But first we must measure it. While I dig the hole, run to my brother Cassim's house and borrow his weighing pan — but remember, say nothing more.'

Cassim's wife was very curious to know what Ali Baba could possibly have that was worth measuring, so she placed some suet on the bottom of the pan. When it was returned to her, she was astonished to find a piece of gold stuck to the suet. She became jealous and angry, and said to her husband, 'Your brother Ali Baba is so wealthy he does not just *count* his gold. He has to *measure* it, like grain! He pretends to be poor, but he must be richer than all of us.'

When he saw the scales and the gold coin, Cassim, too, grew jealous and angry. He ran to his brother's house, and was just in time to see him putting the last of the gold into the hole. And so Ali Baba had to tell his brother the whole story.

REMBLING with excitement, the greedy Cassim cried, 'In the morning I will go to the cave myself — with *ten* donkeys. I will be richer than you!'

'Be careful, brother,' warned Ali Baba. 'If the forty thieves catch you they will surely kill you.'

Cassim soon found the rock and, saying the magic words, opened up the cave and fell upon its treasure. He piled the gold into sack after sack. But when the time came for him to leave, he could not remember the magic words. '*Open, Barley!*' he cried in panic, but of course nothing happened. He tried again and again. '*Open, Rye! Open, Caraway!*' But it was no use. He was now a prisoner.

Later that day the forty thieves returned. When they saw the ten donkeys tied up outside the cave, they knew that someone had discovered their secret. With swords drawn, they rushed inside and killed Cassim without mercy, and cut him into six parts.

'We will leave his body inside the cave,' said the robber chief, 'as a warning to anyone else who might be foolish enough to try to steal our treasure.'

S THE DAY WORE ON, Cassim's wife, waiting at home, grew more and more worried. When her husband did not return that night, she ran weeping to Ali Baba to ask for his help.

In the morning he went to the cave, where he found the remains of Cassim's body, which he brought back in a sack. When he arrived at his own house he called for his servant, Morgiana, an orphan who had been raised as a daughter by Ali Baba and his wife. She had grown into a brave and wise woman, and knew how to solve problems of all kinds.

Ali Baba told her of the terrible fate which had overtaken his brother and said to her, 'While I go to break the sad news to his widow, you must think of some way in which we can bury these six pieces so that people will think that Cassim died a natural death. Otherwise everyone will learn our secret and then the robbers will come and murder us all.'

'I will try,' she promised.

HE NEXT DAY Morgiana went to the workplace of an old cobbler and said, 'Look Mustapha, here is a gold coin. For this I want you to bring your needle and thread and come with me. But first I must bandage your eyes, for you must not know where you are going.'

This she did, and led him through the streets and down into the cellar of Ali Baba's house, where she removed the blindfold. Giving him another gold coin, she said, 'I wish you to sew the pieces of this body together. If you work quickly, and well, you shall have another gold coin.'

When he had finished, Morgiana led Mustapha back to his shop and paid him as arranged. 'Remember, you must tell nobody what you have done or where you have been,' she warned him.

Cassim was then buried properly, all in one piece, and nobody suspected how he had really met his death.

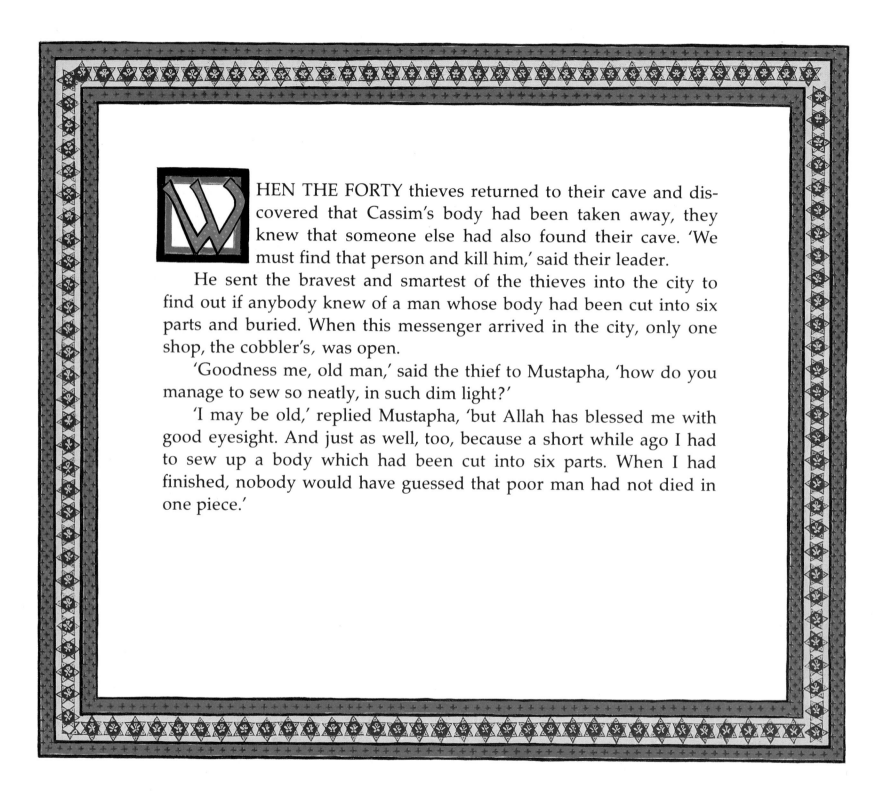

WHEN THE FORTY thieves returned to their cave and discovered that Cassim's body had been taken away, they knew that someone else had also found their cave. 'We must find that person and kill him,' said their leader.

He sent the bravest and smartest of the thieves into the city to find out if anybody knew of a man whose body had been cut into six parts and buried. When this messenger arrived in the city, only one shop, the cobbler's, was open.

'Goodness me, old man,' said the thief to Mustapha, 'how do you manage to sew so neatly, in such dim light?'

'I may be old,' replied Mustapha, 'but Allah has blessed me with good eyesight. And just as well, too, because a short while ago I had to sew up a body which had been cut into six parts. When I had finished, nobody would have guessed that poor man had not died in one piece.'

**T**HE ROBBER could hardly believe his luck. 'I will give you five gold coins if you will show me where you performed such a marvel,' he pleaded.

'I cannot be sure of the direction, for I was led there blindfolded,' Mustapha replied. 'Perhaps if I were blindfolded once more I might be able to lead you there by the sense of touch alone.'

And so, bandaged afresh, he was able to find the way to Ali Baba's house with little trouble — and was well pleased with his reward. The delighted robber placed a mark on the door with a piece of white chalk and, sending Mustapha back to his shop, hurried away to the forest to tell his leader of his success.

SHORTLY AFTERWARDS, when the servant Morgiana returned from the market, she saw the white mark on her master's door. Suspecting this to have been placed there by some unknown enemy, she fetched some chalk and marked all the other doors in the street in exactly the same way.

When the robber returned to the city with his comrades, he was dismayed to find how easily he had been tricked. 'I must be dreaming,' he cried. 'I marked only one door and now I cannot tell which one it was.'

The robber chief was so angry that, as soon as his men returned to the forest, he cut off the unfortunate messenger's head. He now sent another thief into the city to find Mustapha, who was able to find the door of Ali Baba's house once again. The robber marked this door with red chalk, but later, when the thieves came two by two into the city, they found that the clever Morgiana had made identical marks on the doors of all the houses in the street. Therefore, they returned to the forest and cut off the head of the second messenger.

THE ROBBER CHIEF now decided to do the job himself. With Mustapha's help, he soon found the house but, instead of marking it, he memorised its every detail so that he could find it again, even in the dark. Then he returned to the forest and told his comrades of his plan to murder all who lived in that house.

A few nights later, disguised as an oil merchant, he arrived at Ali Baba's house with nineteen donkeys, each of which carried two large jars. Only one of these jars had oil in it. All the rest concealed the thieves, one to each. The robber chief asked Ali Baba if he would be kind enough to allow him to rest his animals for the night in his courtyard, as he was a stranger in the city and had nowhere to sleep.

Ali Baba did not recognise the robber chief and, being a generous man, he offered the oil merchant the hospitality of his house. The donkeys were unloaded and fed, and Morgiana was asked to prepare a meal for the guest.

LATER THAT NIGHT the robber chief returned to the courtyard and whispered to each of his men in turn, 'Stay hidden until I throw some pebbles from my window into the yard. This will be the signal to climb out of your jar and kill everybody in the house.'

Still later that night, Morgiana was working in the kitchen, when the oil lamp began to go out. As there was no more oil in the house, she decided to borrow a cupful from one of the merchant's jars. Just as she was about to remove the lid of the first jar, she was surprised to hear a voice come from inside it, asking, 'Is it time to come out yet?'

Understanding the situation at once, the clever Morgiana whispered, 'No, not yet.'

As she went from jar to jar, she heard the same question and gave the same answer, until she came to the one jar which contained the oil.

ORGIANA took enough oil from this jar to fill all the kettles in the house. She placed these on the kitchen fire and brought them to the boil. Then she carried the kettles into the courtyard and poured their contents into each of the pots in turn. The oil was so hot that the robbers were killed instantly, before they could cry out.

At midnight, when the robber chief threw his pebbles from the upstairs window, he could not understand why his men did not spring from their jars, waving their swords. Thinking they must have fallen asleep, he crept into the courtyard to awaken them. When he discovered that his companions were all dead, he fled at once to the forest to work out a new plan of revenge.

In the morning, Morgiana told her master what she had done. Ali Baba was so grateful to her that he made her his chief housekeeper. Then, with the help of another servant, he dug a great pit in his garden and buried the thirty-seven bodies, and life returned to normal once more.

ONE DAY Ali Baba's son, who now looked after Cassim's old shop, said to his father, 'I have recently become acquainted with a merchant who is new to the market. I have shared a midday meal with him five times without returning his hospitality. Perhaps we could hold a fine feast in his honour.'

Thus it was that the robber chief, disguised in a long beard, came to be invited to eat in the house of the man he planned to kill. The moment she saw him, however, the wise Morgiana guessed who he really was and why he had come — especially when she noticed a dagger partly hidden in the folds of his robe.

After all had eaten, Morgiana appeared before the company, dressed as a dancer, and offered to entertain them. Everyone was captivated by the beautiful girl and her curious dance, which involved the use of a small dagger. However, delight soon turned to horror when, advancing towards the robber-guest, Morgiana suddenly plunged the dagger into his heart.

Ali Baba cried out in disbelief, 'Morgiana! What have you done? This man was an honoured guest in my house. We shall be ruined forever.'

ASTER, I have saved your life,' replied Morgiana. 'Your guest was none other than the robber chief, who came here to kill you.' So saying, she removed the false beard from the dead man's face and pointed to the dagger hidden in his robe.

When Ali Baba saw that his guest was indeed the oil seller and captain of thieves, he realised that Morgiana had saved his life yet again. Overcome by joy, he cried, 'Morgiana, my child, my daughter, will you be my daughter in very truth and marry this handsome young man, my son?'

The wedding took place that very day and there was much feasting and rejoicing in the house.

In time, Ali Baba revealed the secret of the cave to his son, and his son to his son, and they shared their riches wisely and generously, so that Allah blessed them, every one, and the whole city loved and honoured them dearly for the rest of their days. ◡

*For Nico and Tamity Tim*

First published in Australia in 1988 by Walter McVitty Books

This edition first published in 1989 by the Press Syndicate of the University of Cambridge
The Pitt Building, Trumpington Street, Cambridge CB2 1RP
Text copyright © Walter McVitty, 1988
Illustrations copyright © Margaret Early, 1988

Printed in Hong Kong by South China Printing Company
ISBN 0-521-37358-1